A TRUE BOOK

W9-DDQ-280

Muhammad Ali

JOSH GREGORY

Children's Press®
An Imprint of Scholastic Inc.

Content Consultant
James Marten, PhD
Professor and Chair, History Department
Marquette University
Milwaukee, Wisconsin

Library of Congress Cataloging-in-Publication Data
Names: Gregory, Josh, author.
Title: Muhammad Ali / by Josh Gregory.
Description: New York : Children's Press, an imprint of Scholastic Inc., 2017. | Series: A True Book |
   Includes bibliographical references and index.
Identifiers: LCCN 2016031809| ISBN 9780531221709 (library binding) | ISBN 9780531223185 (paperback)
Subjects: LCSH: Ali, Muhammad, 1942-2016—Juvenile literature. | Boxers (Sports)—United States—
   Biography—Juvenile literature. | Political activists—United States—Biography—Juvenile literature.
Classification: LCC GV1132.A4 G74 2017 | DDC 796.83092 [B] —dc23 LC record available at
https://lccn.loc.gov/2016031809

© 2017 Scholastic Inc.
All rights reserved. Published in 2017 by Children's Press, an imprint of Scholastic Inc.
Printed in China 62
SCHOLASTIC, CHILDREN'S PRESS, A TRUE BOOK™, and associated logos are trademarks and/or registered trademarks of Scholastic Inc.
5 6 7 8 9 10 R 26 25 24 23 22 21

Scholastic Inc., 557 Broadway, New York, NY 10012.

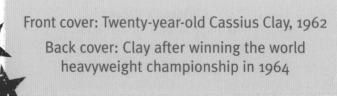

Front cover: Twenty-year-old Cassius Clay, 1962

Back cover: Clay after winning the world heavyweight championship in 1964

Find the Truth!

Everything you are about to read is true *except* for one of the sentences on this page.

Which one is **TRUE**?

T or F   Muhammad Ali never lost a boxing match.

T or F   Muhammad Ali was the first boxer to win the world heavyweight championship three times.

Find the answers in this book.

Contents

THE **BIG** TRUTH!

Refusing to Fight

Ali meets
with reporters

George Foreman and Ali

Ali with the Olympic Torch in 1996

When he was 12 years old, Cassius Clay found a new passion that would change his life.

CHAPTER 1

Birth of a Legend

Twelve-year-old Cassius Clay was sad and angry when he found out his beloved bicycle had been stolen. The red-and-white Schwinn had been a gift from his parents. Cassius told a police officer about the theft. Fighting back tears, he declared that he would find the thief and beat him up. But the police officer had a better idea.

 Cassius was named for a military commander who worked against slavery in the 1800s.

The Start of Something Big

The police officer, a man named Joe Martin, happened to be a boxing coach in his spare time. He told Cassius that he should learn to fight before he went around threatening people. Martin offered to give the boy boxing lessons at a local gym. Cassius took him up on the offer, marking the beginning of a legendary boxing career.

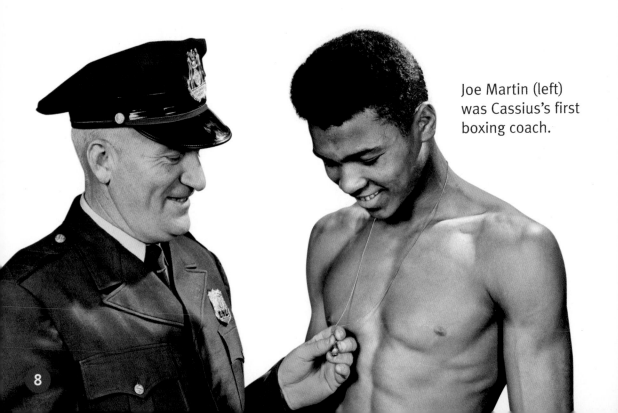

Joe Martin (left) was Cassius's first boxing coach.

Rudy Clay (left) sits next to his big brother, Cassius.

Growing Up in Louisville

The man we now know as Muhammad Ali began life as Cassius Marcellus Clay Jr. He was born on January 17, 1942, in Louisville, Kentucky. His father, Cassius Sr., worked as a sign painter. His mother, Odessa, cooked and cleaned for a living. Cassius also had a younger brother named Rudy, who was born in 1943, about a year after Cassius.

Many public places had separate facilities for white and black people, from waiting rooms to drinking fountains.

Growing up as a black person in the southern United States during the 1940s and '50s, Cassius experienced a great deal of **racism**. In many parts of the country, **segregation** was still legal. Black people were not allowed in many public places and had no access to some of the best schools and jobs. In addition, white people often treated their black neighbors as though they were not equal.

Racism had a big effect on Cassius. He was especially upset when he learned in the news about the death of a 14-year-old named Emmett Till. Emmett was from Chicago, but in 1955 he visited family in Mississippi. While there, he was murdered by a group of white men because he spoke to a young white woman. At the time, Cassius was about the same age as Emmett. Cassius dreamed of fighting against racist acts like this one.

Emmett Till poses for a photo with his mother around 1950.

Cassius (left) trains with a friend at the gym in 1959.

A Natural in the Ring

Joe Martin quickly recognized that Cassius had a talent for boxing. Still, Cassius had to work hard. A match lasted 4 to 15 rounds, and Cassius would have to win the most rounds to win the match. He trained six days a week, running in the morning and working out at the gym late into the night. He jumped rope to become strong and fast. Boxing against his reflection in a mirror helped improve his reflexes.

The work paid off. Cassius won his first **bout**, or boxing match, six weeks after starting his training. At just 14 years old, Cassius won the Golden Gloves, a national **amateur** tournament. He won again three years later. By the age of 18, Cassius had won 100 amateur fights and lost only eight. A lot of his focus was on boxing, and this may have hurt his schoolwork. Yet in 1960, Cassius graduated high school and headed to Rome, Italy, to compete in the Olympic Games, the biggest competition for amateur boxers. This was just the beginning of his career.

Boxing matches occur in a boxing ring, often just called "the ring."

Cassius celebrates a victory in 1960.

CHAPTER 2

Going Pro

As part of the U.S. boxing team in Rome, Cassius Clay continued adding wins to his record. He won his first three Olympic bouts. When he faced off against Poland's Zbigniew Pietrzykowski for the championship, he won again. For his victory, Clay was awarded a gold medal. He had reached the peak of amateur boxing. It was time to move on to something bigger.

Clay had to take an airplane to Rome even though he was deeply afraid of flying.

Back at Home

In Louisville, Clay was honored with a parade to celebrate his Olympic victory. Many people saw him as a hero. However, even this incredible achievement did not stop racism from affecting his life. Not long after returning home, Clay was refused service at a "whites-only" restaurant. Like other black citizens, Clay was judged by the color of his skin.

Though some people treated Clay badly after his return from the Olympics, he was a hero to many others.

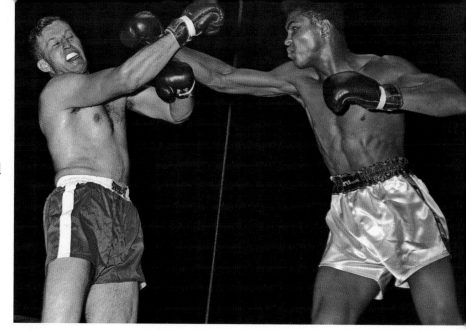

Clay throws a punch at his opponent in his first professional boxing match.

The Next Steps

At home, Clay continued to train. He knew he was ready to become a professional boxer. However, he couldn't begin his career without help. He signed a contract with the Louisville Sponsoring Group. This group of 11 wealthy white men would arrange Clay's fights, cover his training costs, and manage his career. In exchange, they collected half the money he won at each fight. At the time, this deal was considered fair.

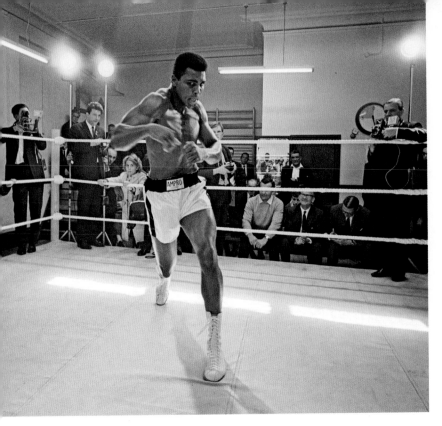

People watch Clay train before a fight. He became known for his fancy footwork.

On October 29, 1960, Clay won his first-ever professional bout. Audiences were amazed by his thrilling, unusual fighting style. He danced around the ring with quick foot movements and struck opponents with fast punches. He was also able to stay standing even after taking heavy punches. Clay himself said that his style was to "float like a butterfly, sting like a bee."

Clay received plenty of attention outside the ring, too. He was charming and handsome. He boasted about himself and insulted his rivals with colorful and witty language. "I'm so fast that last night I turned off the light switch in my hotel room and was in bed before the room was dark," he claimed. He once told an opponent, "If you even dream of beating me, you'd better wake up and apologize."

One of Clay's nicknames was the Louisville Lip, a reference to his trash talking.

The Greatest

Clay won 19 fights in a row to start off his pro career. Fifteen of these victories were **knockouts**. That meant Clay knocked his opponents down and they could not rise within a certain time. However, many boxing experts believed Clay wasn't as good as he claimed. They argued that he only fought boxers who wouldn't give him a real challenge. Clay would soon prove his doubters wrong.

Clay's fame grew with his string of victories. The Beatles even stopped by Clay's gym during their first visit to the United States in 1964.

Some people predicted Clay had only a one in eight chance of winning against Sonny Liston.

On February 25, 1964, when Clay was 22 years old, he faced off against Sonny Liston in Miami, Florida. Liston was boxing's world **heavyweight** champion. Very few people believed Clay could beat him. This didn't discourage Clay. As usual, he bragged about his skills and taunted his opponent in the days leading up to the fight.

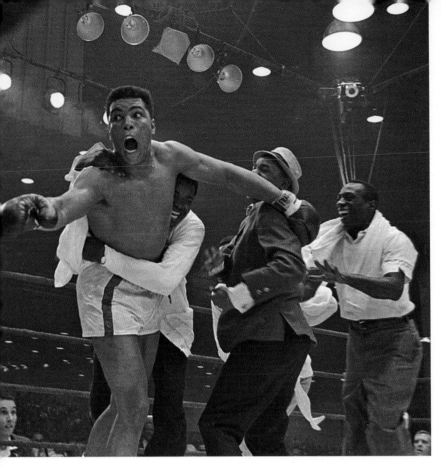

Clay's ringside team holds him back as he celebrates his victory over Liston.

During the fight, Clay proved that he could back up his tough talk with action. After six rounds, Liston could take no more. He gave up, and Clay was declared the winner and the new world heavyweight champion, or champ. From the center of the ring, Clay raised his arms and shouted, "I am the greatest!"

A New Name

Soon after his victory over Liston, Clay announced he belonged to the Nation of Islam. This religion is based on Islam and focuses on pro-black teachings. After a lifetime of racism, Clay identified with the religion. People who convert to the Nation of Islam often take new names. The Nation of Islam's leader, Elijah Muhammad (pictured, left), gave Clay his new name on March 6, 1964. From then on, he was Muhammad Ali.

Life as a Champion

As the world heavyweight champion, Ali had to continue winning to defend his title. In fight after fight, he defeated many of the world's top boxers. On May 25, 1965, he fought a rematch against Liston. This time, his victory was even more amazing. Ali beat Liston with a knockout in the first round of the fight.

Ali had fans all around the world. Here, he signs autographs at a school in London, England.

Malcolm X (left) was a leader in the Nation of Islam when Ali joined. Malcolm X later left the Nation but remained a devout Muslim and a leader in the civil rights movement until he was killed in 1965.

Around this time, Ali's religious and political beliefs began playing a bigger role in his life. He used his fame to speak out against racism. He began working with **civil rights** leaders such as Malcolm X and Martin Luther King Jr. In 1966, Ali left the Louisville Sponsoring Group. He hired Elijah Muhammad's son Herbert as his new manager.

Refusing to Fight

In the 1960s, the United States began fighting a war in Vietnam. To gather soldiers, the U.S. military used a **draft**. Any man who was healthy and the right age could be legally required to join the military. In 1967, Ali was drafted. However, he made headlines by refusing to go. He was a "conscientious objector." In other words, he refused to go to war because of moral or religious beliefs.

WHY ALI REFUSED TO BE DRAFTED

Ali argued that Islam is nonviolent. As a Muslim, he felt he should not join the military. He also explained that the United States treated the Vietnamese unfairly, just as it treated black Americans unfairly. He believed that continued war in Vietnam could not bring equality or justice to either group.

HOW PEOPLE FELT ABOUT ALI'S ACTIONS

Ali was banned from boxing in the United States and stripped of his heavyweight champion title. A court also **sentenced** him to five years in prison and fined him $10,000. Some people thought Ali was unpatriotic. Others saw him as a hero for speaking out.

WHAT ALI DID NEXT

Ali **appealed** his sentence, asking the courts to reconsider their decision. He would not have to go to jail during this time, unless the courts decided against him. Then in 1970, the U.S. Supreme Court recognized Ali as a conscientious objector and reversed his sentence. Ali never had to serve jail time. State organizations also started giving him permission to fight again. Ali's name was cleared, and he returned to the ring.

Joe Frazier walks
away after knocking
Ali to the ground.

CHAPTER 3

Making a Comeback

In October 1970, Ali returned to the boxing ring after three long years. Though he won his first two fights, it was clear that he was out of practice in the often brutal sport. On March 8, 1971, he fought Joe Frazier. During Ali's time away from boxing, Frazier had become the new heavyweight champ. He defeated Ali that night in a 15-round match. It was the first loss of Ali's pro career.

Both Ali and Frazier were undefeated in their professional careers before the fight.

Back to the Top

Over the next few years, Ali worked hard to return to his former glory. He won most of his fights and improved his skills. In 1974, he defeated Frazier in a rematch. By this time, Frazier was no longer the heavyweight champ. So Ali did not reclaim his title by winning the fight. However, he had proven that he deserved another shot at being the greatest.

Ali holds up a fake wanted poster mocking Frazier and predicting Frazier's loss before their 1974 match.

on the floor of the ring after Ali knocked him out

In October 1974, Ali faced the world heavyweight champion George Foreman. The fight took place in Zaire (today known as the Democratic Republic of Congo). Foreman was known for his hard punches. To fight him, Ali used a strategy he called "rope-a-dope." He spent much of the fight avoiding Foreman's punches and leaning against the ring's ropes to save energy. Once Foreman was tired, Ali sprang forward and knocked him out. Ali became the champ again.

People were excited about the rematch between Ali and Frazier. The bout was featured in an issue of *The Ring* magazine.

The Thrilla in Manila

In October 1975, Ali met Joe Frazier for a third and final bout. Before the fight, Ali did his usual controversial trash talking. He said the fight would be a "killa and a thrilla and a chilla when I get that gorilla in Manila."

The fight was long and hard for both fighters. However, it was Frazier who gave up after the 14th round. Ali had defeated his rival once again.

Third Chance to Be Champ

Ali began 1978 as the world heavyweight champ. That changed when he fought a young, inexperienced boxer named Leon Spinks in February. It was only Spinks's eighth fight as a pro boxer. However, he unexpectedly won a close victory over Ali in a 15-round fight and took the championship title. It looked like Ali's greatest years as a boxer were behind him.

Leon Spinks raises his hands in celebration after defeating Ali.

Ali waits in his corner between rounds in his second fight against Spinks in 1978.

However, Ali got a chance to make up for his defeat later that year in a rematch with Spinks. The fight lasted 15 rounds. This time, he managed to defeat his young opponent and reclaim his championship title. The victory made Ali the first boxer ever to win the world heavyweight championship three times. A few months later, in June 1979, he announced his retirement from boxing. He was 37 years old.

The End of an Era

Ali's first retirement didn't last long. In October 1980, he returned to fight Larry Holmes, who had become the world heavyweight champ. Out of practice and well past his prime, Ali lost when he was knocked out for the first and only time in his career. He fought once more, in December 1981. That bout resulted in another defeat. Shortly after, Ali retired for good at the age of 39.

Ali dodges during his 1980 fight against Larry Holmes.

Larry Holmes trained with Muhammad Ali during the 1970s.

Ali received the World Sports Award of the Century for martial arts in 1999.

CHAPTER 4

Life Outside the Ring

In 1984, Ali announced that he had Parkinson's disease. This brain disease may have resulted from the many head injuries Ali received as a boxer. As it progresses, Parkinson's makes it difficult for people to control their movements. People with Parkinson's can also shake uncontrollably and may have trouble speaking. But Ali didn't let the disease stop him from doing great things.

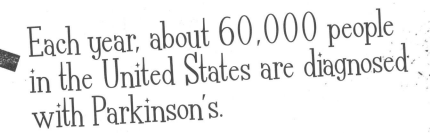

Each year, about 60,000 people in the United States are diagnosed with Parkinson's.

Helping Out

After retiring, Ali worked to raise awareness about Parkinson's disease. He also continued to speak out about racism and other social issues. He became involved in **philanthropy**, too. He traveled around the world to visit poor and war-torn countries. In 1990, he even met with Saddam Hussein, who was then the leader of Iraq. He went without U.S. government support or approval. However, Ali successfully negotiated for the release of 15 Americans being held hostage there.

Timeline of Important Moments

1954

Cassius Clay's bike is stolen and a police officer recommends he learn boxing.

1960

Clay wins the gold medal for boxing in the light heavyweight division.

1964

Clay beats Sonny Liston to become the world heavyweight champ. Days later, he changes his name to Muhammad Ali.

A Large Family

Ali's retirement gave him more time to spend with his family. He was married four times throughout his life. These marriages led to seven daughters, two sons, and many grandchildren. One daughter, Laila, followed in her father's footsteps and became a pro boxer. Ali married his fourth wife, Lonnie, in 1986. The couple stayed together for the rest of Ali's life.

1967

Ali refuses to be drafted into the army.

1978

Ali wins against Leon Spinks in a rematch to reclaim his title for the third time.

1984

Ali announces that he has been diagnosed with Parkinson's disease.

Honored as a Hero

In 2005, President George W. Bush awarded Ali the Presidential Medal of Freedom. The medal is one of the highest honors a U.S. citizen can receive. Other recipients have included civil rights leaders such as Martin Luther King Jr. and Rosa Parks, and filmmakers such as Steven Spielberg and Walt Disney. Decades after battling the U.S. government over the Vietnam War, Ali was honored as one of the country's greatest heroes.

Muhammad Ali kisses the cheek of a young student in Kabul, Afghanistan. Ali is considered a hero for his work to promote peace around the world.

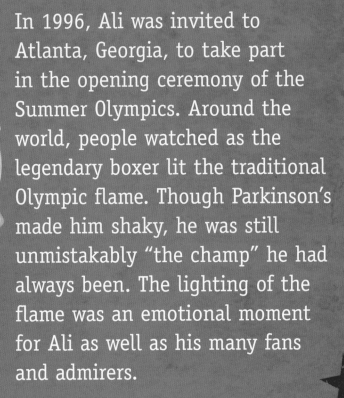

A Return to the Olympics

In 1996, Ali was invited to Atlanta, Georgia, to take part in the opening ceremony of the Summer Olympics. Around the world, people watched as the legendary boxer lit the traditional Olympic flame. Though Parkinson's made him shaky, he was still unmistakably "the champ" he had always been. The lighting of the flame was an emotional moment for Ali as well as his many fans and admirers.

After Ali's death, many people left flowers, pictures, and other tokens outside the Muhammad Ali Center, a museum and cultural center in Louisville, Kentucky.

Remembering a Legend

On June 3, 2016, Ali died at age 74 near his home in Scottsdale, Arizona. Around the world, people mourned the loss of a great man, and many shared memories and paid tribute to his remarkable accomplishments. Political leaders such as Barack Obama and Hillary Clinton, as well as fellow boxing legends Mike Tyson and George Foreman, took part in the memorials.

With his incredible boxing record, Ali was guaranteed to go down in history as a remarkable athlete. However, he will be remembered for far more than his skills in the ring. He always stood up for his beliefs and worked hard to bring positive change to the world. He also inspired many athletes, especially young black athletes, and countless others around the world. For these reasons, he will always be known as "The Greatest." ★

Muhammad Ali serves as a hero and an inspiration for his actions both in and outside the ring.

True Statistics

Total wins in Ali's amateur career: 100

Total losses in Ali's amateur career: 8

Total wins in Ali's professional career: 56

Total losses in Ali's professional career: 5

Number of times Ali won by knockout: 37

Number of times Ali was knocked out: 1

Number of times Ali won the world heavyweight championship: 3

Number of years Ali was banned from boxing for refusing to fight in the Vietnam War: 3 years

Did you find the truth?

F Muhammad Ali never lost a boxing match.

T Muhammad Ali was the first boxer to win the world heavyweight championship three times.

WANTED
Muhammad Ali

FOR THE ILLEGAL WHUPPIN'
OF JOE "TRAMP" FRAZIER

$ **REWARD** $

Resources

Books

Buckley, James Jr., and Stephen Marchesi. *Who Is Muhammad Ali?* New York: Grosset & Dunlap, 2014.

Denenberg, Barry. *Ali: An American Champion*. New York: Simon & Schuster Books for Young Readers, 2014.

Doeden, Matt. *Combat Sports*. Mankato, MN: Amicus High Interest, 2016.

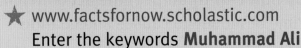

Visit this Scholastic Web site for more information on Muhammad Ali:
★ www.factsfornow.scholastic.com
Enter the keywords **Muhammad Ali**

Important Words

amateur (AM-uh-chur) someone who does some activity for fun rather than for money

appealed (uh-PEELD) applied to a higher level court to a change a legal decision

bout (BOUT) an athletic match or contest

civil rights (SIV-uhl RITES) the individual rights that all people have to freedom and equal treatment under the law

draft (DRAFT) the system that required young men in the United States to serve in the armed forces

heavyweight (HEV-ee-wayt) the heaviest class of boxers, including fighters who weigh more than 175 pounds (79.4 kilograms)

knockouts (NAHK-outs) boxing bouts that end when a fighter is knocked to the ground and cannot rise within a specified time limit

philanthropy (fuh-LAN-thruh-pee) the act of helping others by giving time or money to causes and charities

racism (RAY-siz-uhm) the belief that a particular race is better than others

segregation (seg-ruh-GAY-shuhn) the act or practice of keeping people or groups apart

sentenced (SEN-tuhnst) given a punishment after being found guilty in court

Index

Page numbers in **bold** indicate illustrations.

About the Author

Josh Gregory is the author of more than 90 books for kids. He has written about everything from animals to technology to history. A graduate of the University of Missouri–Columbia, he currently lives in Portland, Oregon.